Chakras

Attain Physical, Mental, And Spiritual Equilibrium Through The Utilization Of Crystal Energy And The Practice Of Meditation To Awaken The Third Eye, A Comprehensive Manual On Kundalini Philosophy And The Yoga Sutra Of Patanjali

Seymour Miranda

TABLE OF CONTENT

Unleashing the Potential of Self-Integration 1

Meditation Through Visualization 11

Everything is Inextricably linked 26

Melatonin Production Should Be Increased 44

Understanding Your Energy 55

Root Chakra healing and balance meditation: 70

Sacral Chakra Healing 81

Manipura represents the Solar Plexus Chakra. 101

Understanding the Interplay of Sexuality and Magick: The Alchemy of Pleasure 116

The Body of the Soul 143

Your Solar Plexus and Personal Pursuits 151

Unleashing the Potential of Self-Integration

Carl Jung, a psychology luminary, bestowed upon us the revolutionary concept of the Shadow self. This complex element of our psyche includes repressed memories, limiting beliefs, and undiscovered bad tendencies. Many of us have mistakenly suppressed these parts in our quest for completeness, expecting to bury them forever. However, Jung demonstrated that such repressed tendencies reappear in various forms, most commonly as denial or projection. This awareness provides a compassionate perspective of why people, especially those who appear self-aware, have elusive blind spots.

The study of Jung's theories can lead to spiritual awakening by revealing significant ideas like the collective unconscious, dream analysis, and synchronicity. Among these enthralling findings is the domain of chakras. However, the critical function of limiting ideas and negative thought patterns in chakra blockage remains largely neglected today.

However, ignoring these deep-seated ideas simply exacerbates the energy impediments since they constantly evade our efforts to hide or evade them. As a result, it's becoming clear that the route to comprehensive healing needs a deep integration of Shadow and chakra therapy. This realization created the foundation of this book: a thorough guide (and notebook!) that merges the principles of the Shadow with the transforming power of chakra healing.

This voyage is much more than a simple chakra examination. It invites you to a profound journey of self-discovery and integration, balancing your energetic flow and cultivating a healthy mentality. We discover the key to a more profound and holistic healing experience by combining chakra healing and Shadow work.

We shall go deeply into the subtle intricacies of each of the seven chakras and their profound link to the Shadow within the pages of this book. You will receive a thorough grasp of all the chakras, the most well-known procedures for healing them, and how the Shadow manifests within each one, revealing the particular obstacles that hamper your personal growth. You will also learn how to avoid the most typical mistakes that new practitioners make while dealing with chakras and their Shadow selves, and you will have the opportunity to participate in practical exercises to heal your chakras using Shadow work.

You will go on a transforming journey with the tools and insights needed to heal and nourish your energy blockages.

The confluence of Shadow work and chakra healing goes beyond cosmetic healing to open the door to your ultimate potential.

So, shall we get started?

Aromatherapy

Every living thing, whether plant, animal, or human, emits a distinct and recognizable odor. The manifestation of their personality, distinctive features, and even their condition of health or illness can be found in these aromas, which are frequently difficult to detect.

Pleasant smells have long been connected with happiness, harmony, and an enthusiasm for life. A healthy newborn baby, for example, emits a mild but distinct pleasant perfume.

When we smell anything good, we inhale deeply, filling our lungs with this life-giving air rich in aromatic chemicals. This energizes and excites us. When confronted with an unpleasant stench, we reflexively hold our breath, sensing that inhaling such a scent adds something harmful and unfavorable to our well-being.

On the other hand, our impression of what is pleasurable or unpleasant is influenced not just by our natural impulses but also by our way of life. A smoker, for example, may find pleasure in the aroma of a cigarette even though it is scientifically shown to be damaging to their health.

Have you ever felt the transforming power of a fragrant incense stick or a fragrant light filling a room? The mood changes, becoming lighter and more relaxed. Our spirits get clearer, and our perception becomes clearer. And, under aromatic essences, we can either leave behind past occurrences or witness them objectively and authentically. This light and transparent sense of joy pervades us, broadening our awareness to include deeper events and a more expansive sense of time.

In other words, aromas influence the depths of our being with their volatile components, going beyond our blocks and processed experiences.

Because the mental, etheric, and non-material forces inherent in plants affect humans' non-material energy bodies, which contain the chakras. However, pure plant essences are required to ensure the synergy between aromatic essences and the chakras. Artificial perfumes lack the activating power of plants and the exquisite intricacy of active ingredients found only in nature.

You can find recommendations for specific essential oils in the chapters dedicated to each chakra. However, remember that the offered lists are suggestions rather than precise relationships. So, when making your selection, trust not just my recommendations but also your intuition and sense of smell.

Apply essential oils to the skin, such as sesame oil or others. Alternatively, place two drops of pure essence on a cotton pad on the corresponding chakra. Prepare all of the cotton pads you intend to use ahead of time. Begin with the root chakra and move your consciousness to the next chakra after a few minutes. Also, remember that you can increase your aromatic experience by burning incense sticks.

Finally, remember that aromatherapy works well with vision meditation, sound treatment, and crystal therapy.

Yoga Exercises

When translated properly, "yoga" means "yoke," implying a connection with the divine to attain wholeness within oneself. Any path that leads to such union can be called "yoga," and these paths can be explored from various perspectives. This broader definition of yoga also includes many meditation techniques.

You'll see that I've linked various types of yoga to each energy center on the following pages. These specific practices uniquely engage and excite the associated chakra, serving as a springboard toward the ultimate goal of unity shared by all kinds of yoga.

If you want to practice yoga or meditation, this can help you choose the best way. Nonetheless, all types of yoga offer efficient ways to cleanse and harmonize the entire chakra system. Also, remember that most yoga practices are better learned from a competent teacher to get the best results.

Meditation Through Visualization

Meditation clears and calms the mind, allowing energy to settle and heal. As we will see in the coming chapters, meditation is generally good but more powerful when used with Shadow work. Holding visualization sessions where you "see" each chakra is an excellent way to heal all your chakras.

However, keep in mind the significance of:

Self-Care

Our physical and energy bodies are inextricably linked, and any disruption in one affects the other. As a result, something as "simple" as self-care can significantly increase the health of our chakras.

To begin with, exercise is a fantastic way to improve energy flow and keep the chakras open. Adopting a healthy and nutritious diet is another excellent strategy to care for oneself. As we will learn later, each chakra is related to various nutrients and dietary groups that can help with healing. Finally, spending quality time taking care of your body and skin or simply doing things you enjoy (such as reading or watching your favorite show) may do wonders for the health of your chakras.

Symptoms of Root Chakra Dissatisfaction

Root Chakra Discord:

When the root chakra is out of balance or malfunctioning, your thoughts and actions revolve around possession and security. Your primary attention is on material possessions, sensory stimuli, and pleasures such as food, alcoholic beverages, and sex, often without regard for the repercussions.

You can also struggle with openly giving and receiving, preferring to protect and limit yourself. This inability to let go and desire to withhold might emerge physically as constipation and obesity.

Overall, your activities are motivated largely by meeting your demands, frequently at the expense of others' needs and neglecting your body's well-being, such as keeping a nutritious diet, adequate relaxation, and a balanced lifestyle. You may cling to specific ideals and aspirations with zeal, rage, or hostility in severe circumstances.

You may suffer bodily and emotional fragility with very limited resistance. Uncertainties in life might weigh heavily on you, and you may feel insecure or detached, as if you are not solidly established. Coping with life's issues becomes incredibly difficult, and you may experience difficulties with assertiveness and stability.

Difficulty connecting with the essential life energy of the Earth through the root chakra, maybe combined with blockages in the sacral and solar plexus chakras, can lead to more serious symptoms such as anorexia or a desire to avoid problems and obligations.

1. A feeling of being ungrounded, dispersed, or disconnected.

2. A sense of disconnection from one's own body.

3. A sense of separation from the Earth.

4. Difficulties with self-care practices such as eating healthy meals and resting.

5. Persistent fear or worry that interferes with daily life.

6. Feelings or thoughts that you are unworthy of being alive.

7. Obsession with material possessions.

8. Aggressive responses.

9. A distorted perception of one's physique.

Fear and insecurity.

Physical signs to look for include:

1. Eating disorders or improper food connections.

2. Substance abuse.

3. Issues with the legs and feet, such as weakness, soreness, or discomfort.

4. Diarrhea or urinary tract infections (UTIs).

5. Persistent weariness, lethargy, or lack of energy.

6. Prostate issues (in men).

7. Knee discomfort or instability.

Lower back issues or chronic lower back pain.

9. Sciatica, or nerve pain in the lower back and legs.

It is crucial to remember that the degree of these symptoms might vary and may be altered by individual circumstances. If you identify numerous signs and symptoms in your life, or if they persist for an extended time, or health professionals who can advise you in dealing with your issues and pain.

Common Errors in Attempting to Heal the Root Chakra

There are some frequent pitfalls to avoid when striving to balance the root chakra:

Ignoring Grounding Exercises: As previously stated, the root chakra relates to grounding and stability. Neglecting grounding techniques, such as grounding visualizations, yoga, or walking barefoot, is an all-too-common mistake. So remember to incorporate these simple techniques into your everyday regimen!

Ignoring Physical Health: The root chakra is also linked to physical health. Physical health neglect, such as bad diet, lack of exercise, or insufficient sleep, might impede root chakra healing. So make self-care techniques that promote your physical well-being as well as your energetic healing a priority.

Fear-Based Mentality: The root chakra is associated with thoughts of safety and security. As a result, clinging to fear, anxiety, or a scarcity attitude can hinder the healing process. Work on letting go of fear and developing a sense of trust and abundance in your life. Affirmations, meditation, and visualization techniques are particularly beneficial in shifting your thinking.

Nature Disconnection: The root chakra is inextricably linked to the natural world. This is why spending too much time indoors or away from outdoors can harm root chakra healing. Make an effort to spend time outside, connect with the elements, and establish a stronger relationship with Mother Earth.

Lack of Self-Care and Self-Nurturing: Self-care is essential for the root chakra. Neglecting your personal needs, failing to set boundaries, and failing to prioritize self-nurturing activities can all impede root chakra healing. This is why you should always practice self-care rituals, set healthy boundaries, and engage in activities that make you happy.

The Darkness The Root Chakra's Aspects
The root chakra and the Shadow are inextricably linked. Trauma and fear both play important roles in isolating

people from aspects of themselves and forming limiting ideas that dominate their lives. As a means of seeking shelter and protection, these events frequently force people to repress some portions of their personalities into their Shadows.

And, as the chakra of dread, the root chakra is particularly linked to the Shadow.

When we have profound traumas or have experienced abuse and neglect, we tend to suppress our emotions into the Shadow, along with our self-worth and limiting beliefs. On the other hand, the Shadow does not remain concealed; as previously said, it manifests in numerous facets of our existence, frequently through projection. It impacts our actions and habits, even if we are ignorant of or deny it.

Consider a child who grew up in an abusive household. As adults, they may have tremendous trouble receiving affection from others and believing they are worthy of love and happiness. Their painful childhood memories remain with them, repressed in their unconscious Shadow. Because of these concealed beliefs, they may join abusive relationships or disregard their health.

In summary, the Shadow traits connected with the root chakra concentrate on worries of future danger (such as reliving past traumas) and the sense that one does not deserve protection or fulfillment. Individuals can begin to heal and restore balance to their root chakra by examining and integrating these parts of the Shadow, establishing a sense of safety and worthiness in their lives.

Unblock Your Root Chakra with These Healing Resources

Numerous approaches and tools are available to aid in the healing and restoration of the root chakra. By applying these approaches, you may improve your foundation and develop harmony in your life. Here are some methods to consider if you want to clear your root chakra:

Nature Interaction

Consider sitting in a lotus or tailor's position on bare Earth and consciously breathing in its aroma to help you build a profound connection with our planet's calming and uplifting energy.

Music Therapy

- Music: Archaic music, particularly from prehistoric societies, contains monotonous and strongly stressed rhythms suitable for activating the root chakra. Even if the original sounds are unavailable, natural sounds, such as recordings of running water or chirping birds, can harmonize this chakra.
- Vowel: The sound "u" corresponds with the root chakra and is in the musical scale's profound C tone. This resonance sets a grounding motion that lowers into your roots, stimulating the ancient earth energies in the first chakra.

Everything is Inextricably linked

As a yoga practitioner—a path that, as previously stated, fundamentally represents the search for oneness consciousness—I find my home in tantric thought and practice. As previously said, many people associate this term with sexuality and sensuality in their broadest sense. This is not unexpected given how many activities with this focus are now available under the umbrella name "tantra."

Such seminars are frequently touted as a means of sexual freedom or just improving one's sex life, and many of them undoubtedly fulfill this objective. This is not what classical, spiritual Tantra is about, even though sensuality and bhoga—pleasure - are key components of many tantric rituals and are not limited to the realm of sexuality.

As a spiritual path, Tantra is concerned with harnessing our sensually experienced reality to achieve spiritual experience and, eventually, enlightenment. At least in its original form, Hatha yoga is a type of tantric path that works with the physical body and our natural subtle energies.

Tantra's approach strives to use the experiencing world as a stepping stone to enlightenment.

There are numerous tantric paths in India, sometimes split into left-handed and right-handed Tantra. Left and right have distinct meanings in this cultural environment; hence, in the classical yoga that arose from it, The left is feminine, whereas the right is masculine. The left is passive or receiving, whereas the right is active or giving. However, left is frequently understood as "dirty" and right as "clean" due to using hands, such as while using the restroom.

Only the "left-handed" tantric schools include in their practice the actual breach of societal or religious taboos. However, I have studied a fundamental concept of all tantric directions more closely so that I do not feel constrained by dogmas and over-regulations.

The principle of the feminine is important to tantric philosophy.

Tantra began as a matriarchal path. This means that the feminine function is viewed as immensely good, both in the shape of women as spiritual gurus and practitioners and in the feminine aspect in all of us.

This is a point of view that sets Tantra apart from all major world religions and most spiritual paths, in many of which the feminine has long been systematically suppressed, and women have sometimes been publicly considered wicked, filthy, and undeserving of spiritual growth.

Thankfully, this has begun to shift in global consciousness in recent decades, but the vestiges of these attitudes remain strong in many areas and far too many minds. Consider that in my own country of Switzerland, women could not vote until 1973!

Other countries were a little earlier in this process, but if we go back 200 years, women's rights were almost nowhere near men's rights anywhere in the world. Through these sad times, Tantra has retained a positive view of the feminine components of creation, for which we are grateful.

However, it would be a mistake to think of tantric philosophy as exclusively focusing on the feminine aspects of life while ignoring our "masculine" side. Nothing is omitted, and everything is included in Tantra. It differs from many religious teachings and approaches in this regard, which appear to want to command and ban a lot, making their adherents feel guilty or even terrified.

This is true not only in the spiritual sphere but also in the vast field of nutrition, where there are ardent supporters and equally zealous opponents of every imaginable nutritional strategy and diet.

On the other hand, Tantra teaches us that instead of wasting energy feeling awful about ourselves and our desires, we should use them to progress spiritually.

As we saw in the previous chapter, letting go of judgment frees up a lot of energy previously used to repress things we shouldn't be doing or feeling. We can use this energy to better understand ourselves and remove the fears and unhelpful ideas at the root of everything we ordinarily judge negatively.

According to the New Testament, we should love our neighbor as ourselves. This is a lovely and worthy notion. But can we pull it off? Certainly not by command. It is tough to love by a command or concept. The continually high divorce rate demonstrates this.

However, the Bible may just attempt to describe what we will be like after we have completely understood and become free.

It is difficult not to be kind and kind to people when we fully grasp that we and our neighbor are one—on——one in the sense that whatever we do to him or her, we do to ourselves, and vice versa! And ideally, this should include ourselves. Many of us who grew up in Christian-based societies continue to do a great deal of harm to our Inner Being because of the concepts of guilt and atonement that are still socially and subconsciously deeply ingrained in the culture in which our basic childhood conditionings were created.

The Pineal Gland's Function

What Is the Pineal Gland and What Does It Do?

It is called pineal because it resembles a pineapple and controls serotonin production. This chemical maintains our circadian rhythm and controls the human body's life cycles.

The pineal gland regulates the effect of light in our bodies. People who understand how to activate the pineal gland are more open to sensations of ecstasy and connection. They may also feel as if they comprehend everything or suddenly understand. Furthermore, when triggered, humans can travel to other dimensions more quickly, often known as astral projection or side observation.

The pineal gland, according to Theosophy, is a source of clairvoyance and intuition and a portal to higher dimensions. The "third eye" allows us to perceive things that are not visible to the naked eye.

How to Turn on the Pineal Gland

Yoga, meditation, and other esoteric approaches can be used to activate. Here's an activity you can do without leaving your house.

- Sit comfortably and mark the point between the brows with your right index finger.
- Pay attention to the sensation of a finger touching your forehead. Feel for heat and vibration at this spot on your brow.
- When you feel the pulsation on your forehead, remove your finger and deepen the sensation in your head.

- Next, imagine a brilliant light shining directly from the top of the head to the throbbing point between the brows and into the skull.

- Pay attention to the sensation of pressure on the forehead where light gathers and enters. Tinnitus and minor discomfort in the forehead, such as pressure, are possible.

This practice stimulates the third eye and helps to decalcify the pineal gland. This exercise should be done regularly or multiple times daily, as desired. You can gradually improve your lucidity in dreams, intuition, and clairvoyance.

Why Is the Pineal Gland Obstruction?

According to researchers, fluoride in water is the primary cause of pineal gland calcification. Also damaging to the pineal gland include chlorine, a low-nutrient diet, processed foods, electromagnetic fields (such as mobile phones), and environmental contaminants.

Pineal gland decalcification activities and workouts

To begin, for this to work, calcium supplements must be avoided. Calcium supplements are the most common cause of calcification. Calcium in industrial food usually comes in one of three forms: calcium phosphate, calcium carbonate, or dicalcium phosphate. So stop eating "all done" and start making smoothies! You'll understand why.

Cacao in its raw form: Because raw cacao is high in antioxidants, it is a good cleanser. It activates the pineal gland, or "third eye," and intuition.

Citric Acid: Lemon juice, freshly squeezed, is wonderful for detoxing your pineal gland.

You can blend this lemon juice with spring water to make something refreshing and less acidic for your teeth.

Garlic: Because garlic dissolves calcium and works as an antibiotic, a garlic remedy is helpful for decalcification. Garlic is also beneficial to the immune system. During your curative treatment, progressively raise your intake to a head of garlic daily! To avoid bad breath, squeeze the garlic and combine it with apple cider vinegar or fresh lemon juice.

Boron is a great detoxifier and cleanser of the pineal gland. It also removes fluoride well. Add 1/4 teaspoon sodium borate (borax) to your green tea. Classic borax, which can be found in most supermarkets, is a cheap source of boron. Borax should be used sparingly, in pure water, with no more than 1/32. The safest and most successful method is to drink this mixture in tiny amounts throughout the day.

Chlorella: Did you know that chlorella has a phytochemical ingredient that can efficiently restore nerve damage in the brain and nervous system? Chlorella is used to treat Alzheimer's and

Parkinson's disease patients. You can live solely on microalgae such as Chlorella and Spirulina, superfoods ranging in size from 2 to 8 microns or the size of blood cells.

The chlorophyll concentration of chlorella is responsible for its green color. It has no processed carbohydrates and a high quantity of digestible protein, fatty acids, non-harmful fats, and chlorophyll. Chlorella is thought to be a perfect whole. In addition to being a complete protein, it contains all of the vitamins B, C, and E, and the main minerals (such as iron and zinc in sufficient amounts to be considered complimentary); it has been discovered that it improves the immune system, improves digestion and detoxification; accelerates healing, protects against radiation, aids in the prevention of degenerative diseases, aids in the treatment of illness, and relieves arthritis pain due to its nutritional

Zeolite: Zeolite is a mineral from volcanic rocks discovered on the ancient seafloor. Its honeycomb-shaped molecules can safely catch and evacuate vast amounts of pollutants through the urinary tract. It qualifies as +++ clay. It is given in high-quality powder manufactured using a specialized micronization process.

For excess calcium, we will also focus on vitamin K2, which functions as a calcium regulator in the tissues, increasing calcium fixing in the bone matrix and cleaning out all the extra deposits.

Avoid all pesticide-containing foods: To detoxify the pineal gland, prepare a remedy based primarily on raw fruits and vegetables, free of pesticides. Pesticides are also present in the meat, frequently occurring when the animals consume cereals or grass. Some people advocate vegetarian diets to detoxify the body or protect the pineal gland from possibly toxic toxins. However, some meats are still advised, so how should priorities be managed?

If you can't pronounce the chemical name, it's probably not good for you. Among these compounds are:

Aspartame and other artificial sweeteners (natural sweeteners such as xylitol are available).

Brown sugar, honey, molasses, agave syrup, maple syrup, or boiled wine may be substituted for refined white sugar.

Deodorants and anti-odor items, industrially manufactured Dental mouthwashes (replace with saltwater, plenty!) Chemical cleaning goods.

Melatonin Production Should Be Increased

Although there is no objective, solid proof, many individuals feel that melatonin aids in fluoride elimination by boosting pineal gland decalcification, which aids in the degradation of existing calcification.

Melatonin is produced by our bodies using tryptophan, an important amino acid derived from the proteins we consume. Melatonin has an anti-aging impact by limiting oxidation in all cellular compartments and increasing the activity of other antioxidant enzymes.

Natural Ways to Maintain a High Melatonin Level

Melatonin is primarily generated at night, and the lack of light boosts its production.

Exposure to as little light as possible at night might diminish or even suppress melatonin levels. Avoid any light source (for example, sleeping with a night light). Melatonin synthesis is disrupted by light. Use a light that filters the blue wavelength if you require a light in the hallway or bathroom. (Light bulbs in yellow).

If you expose yourself to sunlight during the day, melatonin production at night will be favored.

Consume foods that boost melatonin production: Melatonin is made from serotonin, which is made from tryptophan, an important amino acid. As a result, tryptophan-containing foods must be prioritized. What exactly are they?

Tryptophan-rich foods include parsley, pumpkin seeds, cheese, cod, parmesan, milk and soy, turkey, pineapple, eggs, dates, lettuce, bananas, plums, rice, corn, oats, walnuts and hazelnuts, tomatoes, potatoes, and red wine. As a result, it is critical to consume these meals regularly to maintain an adequate serotonin level. Nut eating, for example, increases blood melatonin levels in rats by a factor of three.

The Nettle's Miracles

One hundred grams of fresh nettle leaves provide all of the RDAs for calcium and iron, as well as six times the RDA for pro-vitamin A and four times the RDA for vitamin C. Because of this, nettle should be ingested in the morning or at lunchtime rather than in the evening.

Some components are uncommon, such as choline acetyltransferase, an enzyme that synthesizes acetylcholine, which is found exclusively in nettle. This proves the nettle is not a plant if you are still unconvinced.

Other Fundamental Methods for Beginning Work on Pineal Gland Activation

1. Make the most of both night and day.

A person's sleep schedule and wakefulness must not be disrupted for the pineal gland to develop. The most beneficial sleep routine for the pineal gland is to go to bed early (about 10 p.m.) and rise early (preferably at dawn).

In addition to sleeping in the dark, it is vital to learn how to optimize the benefits throughout the day, preferably by sitting in the sun (or at least near a window).

Electromagnetic fields are your adversaries.

Electromagnetic fields follow us everywhere: we carry them in our pockets (telephones) and use them for leisure and work (computers). Of course, such an impact has a detrimental impact on the development of the pineal gland. Thus, it is critical to take advantage of every opportunity to avoid not only the bustle of the city but also worldly products.

3. Practice meditation whenever feasible.

It has been scientifically established to boost the state of mind and the complete human body, assisting in finding harmony, knowing oneself, and being distracted from the hustle and bustle. Concentrate on the pineal gland, or Third Eye, during meditation.

Chant mantras and meditate regularly. Singing creates nasal resonance, which activates the pineal gland. The more thrilling it is, the more young hormones your body secretes. The sound "OM" is associated with the fourth chakra, the heart's center, and the location of unconditional love. The OM mantra opens the door to universal and cosmic consciousness. You can do it for 5 minutes, 10 minutes, or however long you like.

4. Practice yoga

Yoga devotes special attention to the development of the pineal gland, which is thought to be the same antenna through which our brain perceives the most important information from the outside. Shashankasana, or hare position, is the most beneficial posture for pineal gland growth because it stimulates the pineal gland and higher chakra. This asana can also help with memory and focus.

5. Use crystals such as amethyst, laser quartz, moonstone, purple sapphire, tourmaline, rhodonite, and sodalite to activate the pineal gland and work on Ajna and Sahasrara; in general, any natural stone of blue, indigo, or purple colors can be employed.

Place the stone between your brows for 15 minutes to relax. Close your eyes and try to gaze at it. Maintain your focus for the entire 15 minutes. If you can accomplish this in direct sunlight, the sun's rays will flow through the stone and into the pineal gland. It will also be easier to focus on the light.

6. Use fragrant oils to activate the pineal gland and improve overall mental health.

They also assist with meditation and other disciplines. Using lavender, sandalwood, frankincense, pine, lotus, and wormwood is recommended. Oils can be inhaled, burned in special lamps, sprayed, or mixed into bathwater.

7. Use magnets to aid with detoxifying.

Simply place it between your brows for many hours. They attract alkali, removing calcium crystals from the pineal gland.

8. Ignore alcohol, nicotine, and caffeine.

These stimulants disrupt the body's natural melatonin synthesis system. The less of them you drink, the better for you and your sleep.

Some drugs can interfere with melatonin production; check with your doctor if you are using any of these medications.

9. Get your mind off the new moon.

The new moon is great for new beginnings and pineal gland development. If you empty your mind, you will notice how the pineal gland functions, bringing serenity, balance, and cleanliness to your body. That is why the new moon day in yoga is so significant: yogis are completely dedicated to spiritual practices, not even food and water.

10. Make it a habit to look at the sun for 15 minutes when it rises and again at nightfall every day.

Understanding Your Energy

You may have encountered someone who glanced at you and declared they could see your aura. We are made up of millions of vibrating cells, and when the cells move, energy is produced. Consider this field of energy to be the equivalent of Earth's atmosphere. The aura is the energy field surrounding a living being, although chakras are more detailed.

What Exactly Are Chakras?

The chakras are energy wheels aligning with the brain and other organs. There are seven chakras, with the first placed at the base of your spine and progressing to the top of your head. An emotion, a color, and an element. The seven chakras are as follows:

Chakra of the Root

Solar Plexus Chakra Sacral Chakra Heart Chakra Throat Chakra Third Eye Chakra Crown Chakra

Chakra of the Root

Chakra Sacral

Solar Plexus Chakra, Heart Chakra, Throat Chakra, Third Eye Chakra, and Crown Chakra are all chakras.

The chakra system was originally referenced in the Upanishads, revered Hindu literature from 700 to 500 BCE. Although most focus on the seven major chakras, the body contains 114 energy disks. Each energy flow is referred to as a nadis. A chakra is formed when many nadis cross. Yogic teachings aim to have a balanced chakra system for optimal health. When the chakras are balanced, energy may travel throughout the body and reach the necessary organs.

It's worth noting that each religion's teaching has its chakra system. Various specialists have combined teachings and translations to form the New Age system. For example, the New Age philosophy combines features of awareness and elements, yet ancient Indian teachings do not mention this. We will remain with the New Age system because I believe it is a more holistic, spiritual approach rather than a religious one.

Improperly Balanced Energy Wheels

The chakras might be blocked, underactive, hyperactive, or balanced. No energy can pass through if they are blocked. Underactive indicates that insufficient energy can pass through, whereas hyperactive means too much energy. Because each corresponds to a quality, having insufficient energy can make it harder to convey that quality. Too much of a good thing can take over a person's life.

Physical symptoms typically manifest in the body near the damaged chakra. This might range from self-destructive practices such as bad food and poor posture to specific discomfort in organs and headaches or tension aches. Physical ailments and illness, as well as musculoskeletal difficulties, sadness, and anxiety, can emerge when the chakras are out of balance for an extended length of time.

Because they are all interconnected, when one chakra is out of balance, it can induce an imbalance in the others. When a chakra is out of balance, you may experience physical or emotional symptoms. Each of these will be covered in greater depth in subsequent chapters.

What Are the Benefits of Chakra Balancing?

As you may imagine, balancing your chakras has several health benefits. Some of my personal favorites are as follows:

You can see an overall increase in your health and well-being and heal from physical, mental, and emotional disorders much more quickly.

You can learn how to be more open and observant.

Your memory and focus may improve.

You can feel more optimistic about life without having to fake it, and your creativity can begin to flourish.

You may enjoy a better night's sleep, especially if your stress level is lower.

Your self-esteem, confidence, and sense of self-worth improve.

Why Do We Chant When Chakra Healing?

Buddhists would (and still do) chant to bring more meaning into their lives, following old traditions. They chant the lessons and verses passed down through the years, but it is more than just reciting verses. Chanting relaxes the mind and prepares it for meditation. It's a daily exercise that promotes relaxation, clarity, and concentration.

Bija mantras are chants that are associated with the chakras. Bija means seed in Sanskrit, and these are the most fundamental, single-syllable words that hold the essence of energy. These sounds are used for their unique vibrational frequencies, each directing energy to a different chakra. I prefer to relate chanting to sound therapy because it may sound a little 'out there' to some.

The advantages of sound treatment have been established. Research on fibromyalgia patients found that ten sessions of low-frequency sound therapy reduced pain and improved sleep. Almost three-quarters of the individuals could reduce pain medication (Naghdi et al., 2015).

These seed mantras will be discussed in detail in the chapters dedicated to each of the seven chakras. Before this, there will be more science to help see how chanting can bring healing.

Visualization will help you a lot as you work on balancing your chakras and help your mind stay concentrated. Visualize the energy wheel you're working on as its associated color, and imagine those vibrations traveling toward the center of the wheel while you chant. Visualization may appear to be a bit far-fetched, but the brain cannot distinguish between what is real and what is imagined. Telling your brain that energy is going to the region you want it to flow to can lead to better results.

For many people, entering chakra healing might leave them feeling that something is too good to be true. I completely understand those who aren't yet convinced. That is why we only have one more short chapter to connect the old and modern worlds and look at things from a scientific standpoint.

Chapter 1: Awakening the First Four Chakras

The first chakra is the root chakra.

Muladhara is the official name for the first chakra, and it is formed from two words: Mula, which means root, and Dhara, which means support. This chakra's primary function is to connect all of your energy to that of the Earth. This is referred to as grounding. When studying the root chakra, evaluate it regarding day-to-day living on Earth. Furthermore, the primary job of this energy is to equip you with all you require to survive and have a prosperous life here on Earth. In today's society and time, this concept manifests as emotional and financial security.

This root chakra is red and is placed around your tailbone at the bottom or base of your spine. This chakra also extends to the area beneath your abdominal button.

So, how does this chakra feel? When you are balanced, you will most likely have a strong feeling of accomplishment and personal tranquility whenever you consider shelter, safety, and money. You will also feel deeply linked to your one-of-a-kind human experience. Because this chakra receives so much attention, it may become overactive. As a result, an overactive first chakra will cause high levels of anxiety and a jittery feeling.

These repercussions of being hyperactive stem from fear and a strong will to survive. Indeed, fear's job in our existence is to ensure our survival. This way, an overactive 1st chakra will send frequent reminder messages about survival, even when no threat is present. As a result, many people will experience anxiety as a result of these continual messages of fear. Your body may also experience severe symptoms related to digestive disorders, such as ovarian cysts, hip and lower back discomfort, and prostate issues in many men.

How do you balance the first chakra? From a practical standpoint, you must handle your survival needs first. Fortunately, one of the most significant advantages of this chakra is that it provides enough energy to meet your basic survival demands. After using this energy to the best of your ability, you can begin to quiet and relieve this chakra by focusing on your connection to your spirit. You should set aside time daily to relax your spirit by meditating, praying, or connecting with spiritual guides. Furthermore, performing specific acts to guide and distribute hyperactive energy from your body and root chakra into other energy centers within your body is an excellent approach to constructively channeling bad energy. This can be accomplished by acts of kindness, such as volunteering or devoting your time to serving others with compassion and love.

When the first chakra is underactive, it usually signifies that most of your survival needs have been met; hence, this energy is left latent throughout your body and unused to its full potential. As a result, you may experience "fluid" thoughts or daydreaming throughout your day, as well as difficulty concentrating or the sensation that your mind is "in the clouds," so to speak. Not to mention that you feel "spaced out" during the day since staying connected to your spirit and maintaining a sense of equilibrium in your soul is crucial.

You may need to strengthen your first chakra to feel energetic when you feel divorced from your worldly reality. This is best accomplished by interacting with nature and your surroundings to reconnect with the planet. Swimming and gardening are two hobbies that can activate the root chakra, making you feel more connected to your spirit and more present in the moment.

Root Chakra healing and balance meditation:

Begin by locating a quiet, comfortable location where you can sit or lie down relaxed. Allow your body to settle and your mind to calm by taking a few deep breaths.

Close your eyes and direct your attention to the base of your spine, which houses the Root Chakra. Consider a bright crimson energy circulating this spot, spreading warmth and stability.

As you breathe deeply, visualize roots growing down into the Earth from the base of your spine. Feel these roots extending deeper and deeper, securely connecting you to the core of the Earth.

Imagine taking up the Earth's loving energy through your roots and into your Root Chakra with each inhalation. Feel the energy of security, stability, and strength flooding this chakra. Visualize the red energy brightening and becoming more vibrant with each inhalation.

Release any worries, doubts, or imbalances you may be holding in your Root Chakra as you exhale.

Continue your visualization and breathing exercises, allowing yourself to fully connect with the Earth's grounding energy and the healing energy of your Root Chakra. Pervade your entire self with a deep sense of safety and security.

If you have any specific anxieties or concerns, accept them without judgment and gently release them to the Earth. Have faith in the Earth's stability and support.

Allow the healing energy to flow freely through your Root Chakra by remaining in this state of meditation for as long as it feels comfortable. When you're finished with the meditation, take a few deep breaths and gradually return your consciousness to your physical environment.

Open your eyes and pause to think about your experience. Watch for any changes or feelings in your body, thoughts, or emotions. Carry this sense of solidity and groundedness with you throughout the day.

Remember that regularly practicing this meditation can help heal and balance your Root Chakra, giving you a stronger sense of stability, security, and vitality in your life.

Chapter 1: Introduction to Kundalini Yoga

Before getting into the specifics of Kundalini and its awakening, we must first clarify our conceptions. Comprehension of the book's final chapters necessitates a solid comprehension of Kundalini and its significance. To understand how kundalini awakening activities connect with and influence chakra healing, you must first understand your chakras. This chapter will look at the beginnings of Kundalini and its subsequent applications in the chakras, healing, and daily life. Relax and take in the scenery.

The Origins of Kundalini

Ancient Indians discussed and wrote their kundalini experiences as early as 3,000 B.C.E. Although the exact Sanskrit translation of "little coiled one" is "little snake," the metaphor covers much more. Kundalini represented the ancient Indians' connection to the cosmic, divine force that gave rise to everything. This creative energy, prana, and its manifestation in living things on Earth were dubbed prana-shakti (or shakti).

Shakti, the source of human life, lives at the base of everyone's spine, animating their entire existence. When the coiled serpent (Kundalini) at the base of our spines is activated, it acts as a conduit for the flow of Shakti throughout the body, transforming the individual into a receptacle for the universe's endless potential. Although kundalini practice and recognition were not originally linked to any religion or belief, they became entwined with the gods and goddesses of ancient Indian spiritual tradition.

It fascinates me that Kundalini was not limited to ancient India. Ancient Egyptian civilizations also knew Kundalini, though they named it by different names and connected it with different gods and goddesses. Have you ever wondered what the ankh sign, which appears frequently in Egyptian iconography, means? It symbolizes the combination of male and feminine forces, the divine male and female, for the cause of creation (or the restoration of the source).

The ankh was then worn to symbolize Egyptian pharaohs' spirituality and harmony with the source's potential in their daily rulings and other activities. The lingam-yoni is an ancient Indian symbol for Kundalini, yet another manifestation of the union of masculine and feminine powers. This and other analogies demonstrate that these two ancient civilizations shared a common understanding of such a powerful and influential force.

The ancient Chinese idea of chi parallels the Indian prana, shakti, and Kundalini concepts. However, the terminology employed differs significantly from country to country; what they discuss is consistent throughout cultures. The ancient Chinese believed that we all had a vital power called chi, but only a few could control it.

Chi greatly impacts general health and vigor, but when channeled toward sexuality, the possibilities are virtually boundless. The ancient Chinese understood that diverting orgasmic energy to the brain might promote longevity and halt the aging process and other benefits, just as kundalini-oriented sexual practices emphasize this reversal (see Chapter 3 for more information). Similar to this is the notion of Kundalini, which originates in ancient Indian culture and refers to the realization that a fundamental channel within the body transmits energy from one location to another.

Kundalini reappears in global history with the pursuit of alchemy throughout the Middle Ages. The people were introduced to Kundalini yet again, this time through a technique whose practitioners said they were studying it to transform common metals into gold, albeit with different names and words.

The underlying motivation was buried a little deeper. The underlying aim of these "alchemists" was enlightenment. What is the history of transforming inexpensive metals into precious metals? That was more of a metaphor for the personality work required to achieve higher spiritual harmony.

The more you learn about alchemy, the more you'll see similarities to the Indian spiritual practice of kundalini appreciation. The ancient Chinese understood "orgasm reversal" to signify that the primary procedures of alchemy correspond to numerous means by which an individual might unlock his or her center channel for self-improvement (enlightenment, awakening, psychic powers, and more).

Apart from these global forms, Kundalini has only retained its original name and specifics in its native India, where it was historically fostered by yoga. It took physical movement and meditation to get the little coiled snake moving.

Yogi Bhajan, an Indian yogi who introduced kundalini yoga to the United States in the 1960s, was interested in obtaining enlightenment via the practice without the use of drugs. Yogi Bhajan ignited a firestorm of kundalini consciousness by teaching a type of yoga that values self-discipline and physical enlightenment.

Sacral Chakra Healing

Correspondences

What is the Sacral Chakra, and why is it so important?

The sacrum is not part of your brain or spine but is linked to both, forming a triangle with the two main ones.

When these chakras aren't working properly, it can be tough to live your life as you want to because they're all interrelated, which means that when one is blocked, it can affect everything else. All chakras are vital, but the sacral chakra bridges your physical body and your spiritual self.

Because it permits you to create something new and distinctive, the sacral chakra is the seat of all creativity and imagination. When the sacral chakra is blocked, you lose your imagination and creativity, making it difficult to keep up with what you want to do. When this happens, you may find yourself stuck in one spot or repeating things unnecessarily because you lack the energy or drive to move forward.

The Physical Consequences of a Blocked Sacral Chakra

What effect can a blocked sacral chakra have on your physical health? It can leave you feeling lethargic and uneasy. It's widely assumed that a blocked sacral chakra might lead to male infertility. However, this hasn't been confirmed. Women frequently experience overexcitement or nervous tension when the sacral chakra is obstructed. This could be related to their menstrual cycles because their womb is in the sacral chakra. Heart problems, urinary tract infections, cystitis, and bladder infections are other health issues a blocked sacral chakra can cause.

The Emotional Consequences of a Blocked Sacral Chakra

You will feel disconnected from yourself if your sacral chakra is obstructed. You may feel ungrounded as if you can't be productive or calm no matter how hard you try. Depending on the intensity of your blockage, it may also interfere with your connections with others by making you feel remote from them. There may also be feelings of trying to escape from what is going on in your life since everything feels overwhelming, which is why some people turn to drugs or alcohol as an escape method.

Judgmental thoughts, tension or worry, feelings of isolation, melancholy, or simply not feeling comfortable in your skin.

The Spiritual Consequences of a Blocked Sacral Chakra

Your sacral chakra gives you the ability to be creative and innovative. When the sacral chakra is blocked, your spiritual connection with others suffers because you don't feel like yourself. Feelings of loneliness, perplexity, or even sadness may arise, making you feel even more alone.

You may believe that nothing matters in life anymore and will never be excellent since no creativity or imagination comes from within. There may also be a sense of being too critical of others and believing that everyone around you is worse than you, which we should not tolerate.

What Causes Chakra Blockage?

If your sacral chakra is blocked, it is usually due to a physical cause within your body, just like every other chakra. Dietary imbalance, stress, worry, traditional medical disorders such as kidney stones, bladder infections, chronic illness, or stress from accidents or procedures (all of which can weaken the body and influence the sacral chakra) are examples of these. Bad habits such as smoking, drinking alcohol, not getting enough exercise, or eating unhealthy foods might also be blamed.

When it comes to the sacral chakra, blockages in your mind might emerge due to how you view yourself and the world around you. Poor body image, negative self-talk ("I'm fat," "I'm ugly"), and self-loathing ("Nobody wants to be my friend anymore") are all factors that can prevent you from feeling like yourself.

Also, remaining stagnant in life might make you feel like you're not moving forward, which can cause blockages inside yourself, possibly because you don't like the sense of being stuck in one spot for an extended period.

Anxiety and tension, despair, dissatisfaction with your existing circumstances and relationships, difficulties at work or school, financial difficulties, jealousy, or envy toward others are all emotional causes of sacral chakra blockages. You may also have chakra blockage due to a disconnect with what spirituality means to you or something you feel guilty about and can't let go of.

What Does It Feel Like to Have an Awake and Balanced Sacral Chakra?

Making you happy and fulfilled. You will also be able to bring new and interesting things into your life since you are open to them and they are within your reach. This might involve starting a business or discovering a new method to be creative and productive with your time.

Balance in this chakra usually indicates that you don't have any bad emotions or judgments within yourself, making it simpler to be around others because they bring out the same sensations without generating too much stress. When you have a healthy sacral chakra, you can give and receive love and nourishment from others while fully loving yourself.

You'll be more spiritually open and able to connect deeply with God or your higher power. You'll have a strong sense of purpose, great self-confidence, and a strong desire to make a difference in the world – without being too pushy about it. There will be a greater sense of well-being within oneself, which we all desire in life. We want to feel good about ourselves, and we also want to be able to freely offer and receive love without experiencing any bad emotions.

Individual Chakras (Major) Chapter 5

Comprehending the role of the chakras in each other's operation is critical, but so is comprehending how they work separately. Only by deeply exploring each chakra can you identify which ones you may have blocked and how to unblock them. This will assist you in identifying areas of your life that you believe may be influenced by chakra blockages and will help you develop a better sense of self. In this chapter, we will go over each of the individual major chakras in detail, providing essential information about the aspects of life that each one governs and supplementary information about them and any relationships they may have.

Color associated with the Root Chakra:

The element associated with red:

Body Parts Related to the Earth:

The base of the spine, also known as the pelvic floor, is the point at which the earth and the body come into touch.

Description

The root chakra is the foundation of the entire chakra system. This implies that it exists in a dualistic state. On the one hand, it is the least important chakra because it deals with the lowest aspects of human life. However, it is also the source of many parts of your sense of self, such as your essential identity, origins, and link to your physiological processes. It is an important element of your daily life and your unconscious mind. Some people believe the root chakra represents a more animalistic element of human nature, revealing our primal tendencies. However, this is one of the most dangerous chakras that is out of balance. Because energy tends to concentrate here to rise into the crown chakra, a blocked root chakra means your energy can't even travel up to the next chakra, the sacral chakra. If your root chakra is out of balance, there is a good chance that your entire system is out of balance and lacks any flow. Your higher chakras will be disconnected from their energy source, and you will feel you lack roots and wisdom. Ensuring this chakra is open and flowing freely is critical to the operation of the overall chakra system.

CHAPITRE 4 RELAXATION

Some people engage in sports, fitness, music, or reading. On the other hand, others adopt relaxation activities to alleviate their worry. This part will teach us about two ways to deal with the bodily symptoms of anxiety. Deep breathing and muscle relaxation are two of them.

Exercises in deep breathing

Rapid breathing is one of the symptoms of an anxiety disorder. This can produce dizziness, which increases anxiety and causes quicker breathing. It's a never-ending circle. By practicing deep breathing when relaxed, you will be prepared to do the same when anxiety arises.

The main thing is to practice for around 3 minutes every day until it becomes second nature to you. Deep breathing can also help to alleviate any underlying anxiety you may be experiencing. Take the following steps:

Maintain a consistent rhythm. Make sure you take twice as long to breathe out as you do in. For example, breathing in for two counts and out for four counts.

Try breathing from your diaphragm. When a person becomes concerned, they tend to breathe deeply from the stomach rather than the chest. This indicates that you are practicing shallow breathing, which causes shortness of breath.

Check whether you are breathing from your diaphragm by placing your palm below your sternum. When you breathe, you should feel the top of your abdomen move in and out.

When you breathe, ensure your upper chest and shoulder muscles are relaxed; when you exhale, relax these muscles until you can rely solely on your diaphragm.

Muscular unwinding

This strategy can be used as part of a pre-planned program or at any time of day.

For scheduled times:

Find a comfortable, quiet location with no distractions. Make sure you don't have any other important tasks that can interfere with your work. You can lie on your back or sit in a comfortable chair. Please read the instructions from beginning to end before proceeding.

With your eyes closed, you will work on various muscle groups. You will first contract the muscle as you inhale and then relax it as you exhale.

To begin, concentrate on your breathing for a few minutes before beginning.

Hands: Breathe in as you clench your right hand for a few seconds until your forearm becomes rigid; exhale as you relax the muscle. Rep using your left hand.

Arms: Inhale as you bend your elbow and tense the muscles in your right arm; exhale as you relax the arm.

Face: Frow as hard as possible and briefly lower your brows before relaxing the facial muscles. Raise your brows for a few seconds before relaxing. Relax your jaw once it has been clenched.

Chest: Breathe deeply for a few seconds before returning to regular breathing.

Buttocks: Clench your buttocks together as tightly as you can, then relax.

Repeat this practice four times daily, and you will soon realize your general tension has decreased.

In everyday situations:

Because you cannot execute the following workouts while out and about, you may require some easier approaches that can be performed anywhere. When you are feeling worried, use the following techniques:

Turn your neck as far as possible in both directions, then relax.

Tense your back and shoulder muscles completely for a few seconds before relaxing.

Training in Relaxation

Relaxation training is another technique that can be used to halt a panic episode. When you do this, you can gradually and methodically release the tension you have been carrying. Because the tension may be causing your anxiety, releasing it can usually make you feel better, even if just slightly. By engaging in this exercise, you effectively ensure you can relax before the panic attack becomes too severe.

This can take numerous forms, including progressive relaxation, breathing training, and creative visualization, which will be described in this chapter. The main objective is to inform your brain that you should be relaxing, and when you tell your brain that there is nothing worth stressing over right now, you can hijack and prevent the panic attack from worsening. You may effectively compel your brain to realize reality—the anxiety is unnecessary, and the panic attack will have no effect.

The first step, however, is to learn to not feel frightened when a panic attack is approaching. While this may be tough, if your first reaction to a panic attack is to become fearful of the consequences, you will suffer. Take a few deep breaths and assure yourself that everything is fine. If you have a mantra or an affirmation that helps you stay calm, now is the moment to use it. If not, deep breathing will suffice, and you will have to go on to one of the relaxation techniques.

Manipura represents the Solar Plexus Chakra.

This chakra governs our self-esteem and confidence. It is physically positioned in the upper abdomen. This is a chakra that protects what the swadhishthana chakra has generated. It is represented by the color yellow and the element fire.

To understand how our solar plexus chakra impacts us, consider self-assured persons. These people are usually friendly, generous, and sympathetic. They do not engage in insecure actions because they do not need to prove themselves to anyone else. They are also self-assured when beginning new businesses or meeting new people.

When we have strong self-esteem, we are unaffected by the unfavorable opinions of others. We must have faith in ourselves to preserve what has been created.

People who have stomach problems daily may have an imbalanced solar plexus chakra. Similarly, disorders like heartburn and ulcers may arise as a result of this imbalance. This emotional imbalance can contribute to feelings of powerlessness and insecurity. People who have poor self-esteem may struggle to take control of their lives. They may also avoid social events and any situation in which they may be in the spotlight.

Also, because we don't feel in control of our lives, we may begin to place too much emphasis on others. This might lead to insecurity as we compare our lives to those of others. In severe circumstances, we may even experience acute envy and greed. On the other hand, an imbalanced chakra may result in shows of anger and pride. In your life, you may act out by putting others down or disregarding other people's viewpoints. You may even find it difficult to distinguish between assertive and aggressive behavior. While these actions may appear to be evidence of confidence, they are signs of insecurity.

The solar plexus chakra is associated with both spiritual movement and rest.

This is the single location in the subtle body where all 72,000 nadis converge and redistribute. This signifies that this chakra helps to distribute energy (prana) throughout the body. As we progress from this chakra to the four higher chakras, we move from movement to stillness.

The Heart Chakra is known as Anahata. This chakra is sometimes regarded as a link between the physical and spiritual worlds. This is also the location of complete unconditional love. It is physically placed in the center of the chest, immediately above the heart. As a result, it affects the heart, lungs, and chest.

The heart chakra is symbolized by a figure of 12 petals with an upward-facing triangle intersecting with a downward-facing triangle. This symbol indicates that we are progressing from the lower chakras to the higher ones since the downward-facing triangle represents the physical domain, and the upward-facing triangle represents the spiritual realm. The air element and the color green signify this chakra.

When our heart chakra is in alignment, we feel love for ourselves and others. This is significant because true love cannot be felt outside of ourselves. A balanced heart chakra allows us to be more sensitive toward others. This means we may appreciate and believe other people's experiences, even if they differ. In its purest form, the heart chakra assists us in experiencing and living our lives with Divine love.

When the heart chakra is out of harmony, it can cause bodily difficulties such as heart disease, asthma, other lung diseases, and even weight problems. It can have an emotional impact on our relationships with ourselves and others. In this instance, fear replaces love. When we fear ourselves, we do not allow ourselves to enjoy life completely. We don't spend time with ourselves to figure out who we are, what we want, and what makes us feel complete. In extreme circumstances, we may even experience self-hatred. After all, as we've seen all too frequently in the globe, there's a fine line between fear and hatred.

Regarding our interpersonal connections, we may respond from a place of insecurity. When we meet strangers or people from various circumstances and origins, we may react with anxiety and even hatred. Even in our closest relationships, we may find communicating and behaving with love difficult. A blocked heart chakra can also cause acute emotions of loneliness and isolation. We have no issue connecting with others when our heart chakra is aligned, especially during challenging circumstances. In reality, we may learn to see ourselves as part of a complex life network. On the other hand, a blocked heart chakra may leave us feeling befuddled and out of place in this world.

There's another way this lack of balance can show up in our lives. Sometimes, we suffer because we don't know how to love ourselves first before we can love others. In other words, we may not know how to prioritize and repair ourselves before entering any relationship. We may also struggle to set clear boundaries with individuals we care about and to be open and honest about our needs and expectations. If you find yourself giving too much of yourself and not receiving anything in return, your heart chakra may be out of balance.

To comprehend the spiritual significance of this chakra, we must first define anahata. Anahata means "unstruck" or "unhurt" in Sanskrit. The unstruck sound has no reverb and represents complete serenity and balance. We require complete intellectual steadiness to bring our heart chakra into equilibrium. However, our intellect may be ineffective if emotions do not accompany it. Again, we can see how the balance of intellect and emotion can assist us in exploring the spiritual elements of the heart chakra.

SWADHISTHANA CHAKRA HEALING AND UNBLOCKING S it in a comfortable position. Cross your legs so that one rests on top of the other. Your posture is crucial. When you have the proper posture, the passage of energy through the energy channels is facilitated.

(A 10-second pause)

Your body posture may be one of the reasons why your chakras are blocked or unbalanced. Correct posture is advised not only during the chakra healing meditation process but also in everyday life. Your posture alone might boost your self-esteem. Standing or walking with your spine upright and your head held high will make you appear charming and attractive.

Your psychological condition is intimately related to the position and mudra of your hands. You must pay attention to the position and mudra of your hands when practicing chakra unblocking and balancing.

You can hold your hands in Chin mudra or Dhyana mudra. The fingers and palms should be relaxed.

(A 5-second pause)

The palms of your hands are placed on your lap in Dhyana mudra. The left palm rests on the right. Dhyana mudra aids in the development of concentration. Dhyana is the Sanskrit word for concentration.

(A 5-second pause)

The left hand in Dhyana mudra represents the illusionary or material world. The spiritual world is represented by the right hand resting on the left.

Bring your attention back to your body. You are sitting with your back straight. Your back is straight. Your head is parallel to your spine.

(A 5-second pause)

Bring your attention back to your breathing. Your breath must come from your gut. Feel your belly's expansion when inhaling and your belly's contraction when exhaling. Do not try to hold your breath. With each breath, feel your mind and body relax.

(A 10-second pause)

The Swadhisthana chakra unblocking and balancing practice begins.

Gently remind yourself that you are balancing and repairing the Swadhisthana chakra. Behind the genitals is the Swadhisthana chakra. Energy manifests as sexual energy in the sacral chakra, also known as the Swadhisthana chakra.

(A 5-second pause)

In today's environment, sex has come to represent negativity. People are embarrassed by their sexual impulses and sentiments. When people have sex, they experience feelings of guilt. The majority of us connect sex with sin.

This disrupts the Swadhisthana chakra's balance. People with low libido or sex drive, on the other hand, lack the stamina to pursue their vocations actively. They underperform and lose interest in their work or business. You must strike a balance between your sexual urges and artistic interests if you want to live a happy and harmonious existence.

This is only possible if your Swadhisthana chakra is balanced. Sex is a great energy in and of itself, but in excess, it prevents you from being productive in life. You can effortlessly transfer sexual energy into creative energy by regulating the Swadhisthana chakra.

Water is the element connected with the Swadhisthana chakra. Our mind's creative forces are at work. Water stagnation causes it to smell and become nasty. Similarly, you must allow your creativity to flow in numerous directions rather than focusing solely on sex.

Understanding the Interplay of Sexuality and Magick: The Alchemy of Pleasure

This chapter dives into the alchemical combination of pleasure, sexuality, and magick. Here, we embark on an enthralling investigation of the interplay of these solid forces and how they might be used to spark deep change in our lives.

Consider a world where pleasure is more than a temporary sensation but a portal to spiritual enlightenment and personal progress. We realize in this reality that pleasure is a powerful energy capable of sparking our deepest desires and connecting us to the divine nature within.

To grasp the alchemy of pleasure, we must first appreciate the essence of sexuality. Sexuality is a living force that permeates all aspects of our being. It includes our physical bodies as well as our emotional and spiritual landscapes. It is a language that transcends cultural boundaries and societal rules to communicate our essence.

When we do sexual activities with intention and reverence, we open the door to significant transformation. Sexuality becomes a channel for the flow of energy, a dance between polarities, and a sacred communion that transcends the physical realm's constraints.

On the other hand, Magick is the art of summoning invisible forces to effect change at our command. It involves deliberate manipulation of energy and matching our aims with universal rules. Magick acknowledges that everything is interrelated and that by working with the universe's energetic currents, we can manifest our goals and alter our reality.

We uncover unlimited possibilities in the alchemical union of sensuality and magick. Pleasure transforms our wishes into actual manifestations, becoming the alchemical elixir that powers our spiritual progress. We may transform the ordinary into the remarkable by balancing these enormous forces.

We investigate several facets of the alchemy of pleasure to better comprehend this dynamic. We investigate the powerful influence of pleasure on our physical, emotional, and spiritual well-being. We look at orgasmic energy as a means of spiritual enlightenment and human transformation.

Furthermore, we travel into the realms of sacred sexuality, where pleasure and spirituality become one. We investigate ancient techniques like tantra, in which the weaving of sexual energy becomes a doorway to transcendent realms of consciousness. Tantric techniques teach us how to grow sexual energy, increase our capacity for pleasure, and form deep relationships with ourselves and our partners.

The research of the mind-body link is also part of the alchemy of pleasure. We investigate the transforming potential of mindfulness and intentionality in sexual encounters. We augment the alchemical potential of pleasure by bringing conscious awareness to our desires, sensations, and emotional landscapes, transforming it into a sacred rite of self-discovery and empowerment.

As we move through this chapter, we will look at the role of pleasure in manifesting our desires. We see pleasure as a vibrational match to our intentions, which can help us materialize more effectively. When we link our sexual experiences with our objectives and ambitions, we tap into a reservoir of creative energy within ourselves, unleashing our power to create our dreams.

Join me on this journey into the alchemy of pleasure as we uncover the mysteries of its transformative power. We will learn to accept pleasure as a catalyst for spiritual growth, a tool for manifestation, and a portal to our true selves. Let us embark on this alchemical adventure, where sexuality and magick collide, and pleasure becomes the key to realizing our full potential.

WHAT IS THE ORIGINAL CAUSE?

The root signifies "jad" in Hindi, India's native language. As a result, one is the root cause, whereas the other is heaviness (Stress). In our daily lives, we frequently find that understanding the fundamental cause of an issue relieves its heaviness (stress). This means that the outcome is not the cause in and of itself. The cause is not the real cause of the problem; nonetheless, the reason is the foundation of the problem, and addressing it alters the outcome. What do we aspire to be? What have we become in the absence of this? This is critical to comprehend.

"Where do we want to go?" is irrelevant. "What do we want to accomplish in our lives?"

What is vital to understand is "where we are now in our lives."

This suggests that we can achieve the desired results if we work properly. The result is fake if we work hard in the wrong area or technique. For this, every problem we seek a solution (and if we do not receive one) must be understood and addressed, whether it be a health, financial, or other issue.

Consider a tree; the upper half is densely packed with branches, leaves, and fruits. What we see is the visible portion above ground. Parts of the tree that are beneath the ground are not visible. The inner section, which is the base, is called the root. When a tree is growing, consider the foundation of its growth, which is its roots. When the roots are fed, the upper part develops a healthy existence. The tree's growth will be halted if the roots are not properly nourished.

It is not enough to pour water or spray medicine on the leaves of a dying tree to make it green; this will not prevent the tree from dying. The tree will not be around for long. It is critical to feed the tree's roots; only then will the tree turn green again because the root is the source of its life.

In the same way, let us strive to comprehend the origins of our lives.

Examine a tree by dividing it into three sections: the root, the middle section, and the upper section. It contains three tenses: the root, beneath, is the past tense, the middle part is the present tense, and the top is the future tense. We can see a tree's middle and upper parts, but we can't see the root. If we want to strengthen it, we must focus on the roots rather than the apparent aspects.

Similarly, if we attempt to comprehend man's existence, we will discover that our past is our source. Our present is defined by what is happening right now. Our future is defined by what we desire to be or achieve. We attempt to modify our present and future but cannot change our past. What we call "flavor," "habits," and "beliefs." In English, a well-known proverb says, "Your Nature is your Future." Everyone works hard to make the present and future better. They, however, fail.

Because our flair (nature) is a pattern generated in our past, it cannot be created in the present. And our past is the source of our current existence. People work hard to modify the present to create a better future, yet they cannot change their habits and nature because the source of all our troubles is not in the here and now but in the intangible past.

The man keeps roaming to numerous places due to his lack of information. He will continue to seek therapy for his ailment from a variety of doctors. If his health does not improve in one facility, he will transfer to another, just as he would leave one job and hunt for another. In personal life, a man may divorce one wife and marry another, or a woman may divorce one husband and marry another. But nothing has changed in life.

So, how do we alter our flare or skills (nature)?

Our flair (nature) is the source of all issues in life. We incorrectly create our daily schedules and food routines due to our personalities and habits. Then, we become prey to many diseases such as diabetes, high blood pressure, asthma, obesity, cancer, and so on. People do not trust each other because of their nature (personality). It is also a natural trait to lack confidence.

The question now is, what does flair (nature) mean? In Hindi, the term flair (nature) comprises two letters:'swa' + 'bhaav' ='swabhaav.' 'Swa' denotes self or existence, while 'Bhaav' indicates value (respect). Thus, our true flare (swabhaav/nature) is what we consider ourselves to be, what we regard ourselves to be.

How we perceived ourselves since childhood, how we formed our personalities, and how we fed our thoughts positively or negatively. All of this contributes to our character, which we do not understand. Even if understood, it cannot be changed because it has taken the form of our subconscious mind's roots, which are not physically evident. Today, everyone is tormented by this unnoticed flair (nature). And when we discover and focus on this unseen flair (the source of our being), our lives change. This is the most important point to grasp before further.

The Seven Principal Chakras

The chakra system comprises seven major energy centers that run along the bodies. Each chakra represents a different quality, function, or part of our existence. Understanding each chakra's features is critical for harnessing its transforming power and establishing balance and harmony. In this chapter, we will look in depth at the seven major chakras, learning about their significance and how they affect our physical, emotional, and spiritual well-being.

1. Muladhara (Root Chakra):

The root chakra is positioned near the perineum at the base of the spine. It is the chakra system's basis, signifying our connection to the physical world, stability, and survival instincts. When the root chakra is balanced, we feel anchored, secure, and confident in our ability to face life's obstacles. Imbalances in this chakra can cause dread, insecurity, and physical symptoms like lower back discomfort or digestive problems. Grounding activities, connecting with nature, and practicing self-care are all practices that support root chakra healing.

2. Sacral Chakra (Svadhishthana): The sacral chakra is placed directly below the navel in the lower belly. It is linked to our imagination, pleasure, and emotional well-being. The sacral chakra influences our ability to enjoy pleasure, accept change, and maintain good relationships. It is associated with water and is represented by the color orange. A balanced sacral chakra allows emotions, creativity, and sexuality to flow freely. Imbalances in this chakra might cause emotional instability, creative impediments, or trouble forging personal relationships. Exercise creative

outlets, healthy sensuality, and emotional expression and release to heal the sacral chakra.

3. Manipura Chakra (Solar Plexus):

It signifies our strength, self-assurance, and willpower. Imbalances in the solar plexus chakra can cause low self-esteem, insecurity, and difficulties setting boundaries. To bring this chakra back into balance, engage in activities that increase self-esteem, use positive affirmations, and create a strong sense of self-worth.

The heart chakra (Anahata) is positioned in the center of the chest, at the level of the heart. Compassion and emotional healing. The color green represents the heart chakra related to the air element.

When this chakra is balanced, we feel love and acceptance for ourselves and others, promoting harmonious relationships and emotional well-being. Heart chakra imbalances can emerge as difficulties in giving or receiving love, resentment, or emotional pain. Forgiveness, gratitude, and acts of love and compassion can all be used to repair the heart chakra.

5. Throat Chakra (Vishuddha): The throat chakra governs communication, self-expression, and real voice and is located in the throat region. It shows our ability to communicate effectively and assertively. We can successfully convey our thoughts and feelings, tell our truth, and listen carefully when the throat

chakra is balanced. Imbalances in this chakra can emerge as difficulties expressing oneself, fear of criticism, or a failure to communicate effectively.

6. Third Eye Chakra (Ajna): The third eye chakra is placed between the brows, just above the nose bridge. It denotes intuition, inner wisdom, and consciousness expansion. Intellect and access to deeper insights. Imbalances in the third eye chakra might cause a loss of clarity, trouble making decisions, or a sense of being estranged from one's inner direction. Meditation, visualization, and engaging in activities that excite the imagination can all aid in the balance of the third eye chakra.

7. It represents oneness and enlightenment and transcends individuality. The crown chakra represents the element of thought and is represented by the colors violet or white. When the head chakra is balanced, we feel a spiritual connection, purpose, and increased consciousness. Crown chakra imbalances can cause feelings of alienation, a lack of spiritual fulfillment, or trouble reaching higher realms of awareness. Meditation, prayer, and spiritual pursuits can all help to balance and align the head chakra.

Within our subtle body, the seven primary chakras constitute a powerful system of energy centers. Each chakra impacts several areas of bodily, emotional, and spiritual well-being. We can tap into the transformational potential of the chakra system and experience significant personal growth and spiritual awakening by engaging in practices that heal and balance each chakra, such as meditation, energy healing, yoga, and self-reflection.

EXERCISES AND DAILY PRACTICES FOR HEART CHAKRA BALANCE

As we discussed in the first chapter, having an open and balanced Heart chakra allows you to access deeper qualities of service and love for your community. It is the source of the desire to contribute in whatever form. This is because persons connected to their

Heart chakra have access to unconditional, limitless love and compassion, including what we call Divine love. There is plenty to go around. The more you allow yourself to experience and receive love, the more love there will be for others. With an open and balanced Heart center, we can feel surrounded by love and easily give and receive love.

Begin by focusing on appreciation when working to connect with and open your Heart chakra. Choosing compassion and empathy over judgment and anger is not always simple, but focusing on appreciation can help you connect more to your Heart chakra and access these energies. Consider your perceptions of others, including family members, friends, acquaintances, coworkers, and employers. Are they also blessed by what you wrote in your thankfulness journal? What ancient wounds could they be carrying? What could they be going through in their life or their inner world that is prompting them to act this way? Have you ever done or said anything similar when confronted with a quarrel or an emotional trigger? We typically gain a deeper knowledge of people when we study our inner world. Allow this to be a source of comfort.

— JUNG, CARL

IN ADDITION TO THE GRATITUDE LIST, THE FOLLOWING

EXERCISES/PRACTICES WILL HELP YOU BALANCE YOUR HEART CHAKRA.

- Establish a balanced energy flow in your home. The Heart chakra, as stated in the first chapter, is the "balance point" of the seven chakras, serving as the link between the physical and spiritual chakras. As a result, harmonizing and integrating the body, mind, and spirit is important to the Heart center. We may help encourage this by de-cluttering, cleaning our space, and burning incense, sage, and other cleansing products to create a balanced energy flow in the home.

What Is Kundalini Yoga and What Are Its Goals?

Awakening, balancing, and harmonizing Kundalini energy. Individuals who begin a Kundalini yoga journey frequently say that the awakening symptoms begin after only one or two sessions. This awakening deepens as they progress through their Kundalini yoga journey. This yoga technique also supports Kundalini's energy, keeping it awakened, complete, and thriving in the practitioner.

Yoga of the Kundalini

Not all yoga practices are performed in the same way. Some are designed to stretch the physical body, others to foster a mind-body-spirit connection, and others, such as Kundalini yoga, are designed for specific objectives.

Kundalini yoga does not emphasize the physical as other techniques, such as Hatha yoga. Instead, meditation and mantras are a core aspect of the broader practice. The combined experience of the mind, body, and spirit brought together by these three activities promotes Kundalini awakening and flow. Yoga positions help to support and awaken the body, mantras help to support and awaken the mind, and meditation helps to support and awaken the soul.

Kundalini yoga, which Yogi Bhajan introduced in the 1970s, is still relatively new to the Western world. It is, however, becoming more popular as more people attempt to integrate the mind, body, and spirit link into their lives.

The Corpses

Kundalini yoga is connected with ten bodies. Kundalini yoga awakens all ten bodies, allowing people to continue experiencing full Kundalini flow. These are the bodies listed below.

The Body of the Soul

The soul body is your spiritual flow. This is the point at which you connect with your Soul and infinity. The soul body is your inner self and the foundational body. It allows you to live your life from your heart. This body responds to any type of heart activity and Kundalini energy raising.

The Negative Self

Your negative mind is your second body. This is one of our most powerful bodies since it constantly works to assess the environment and situations you are in, as well as whether or not there is any risk present. This body is responsible for your ability to survive and provides us with what is commonly referred to as "a longing for belonging," a concept used by Yogi Bhajan. Integrity and discipline might help you balance your negative thoughts.

Positive Thinking

Your optimistic mind is your third body. This helps you evaluate pleasant, useful, and affirming in your surroundings and circumstances. This body shows you where opportunities exist and where you might be able to obtain resources. Willpower and playfulness are brought into your life by the playful mind. Everything you do with your navel point, or core, helps you maintain a good mindset. You can also counteract it by improving your self-esteem.

The Mind's Neutrality

Your neutral mind leads you through assessing information from both your negative and positive minds. The compassionate, neutral mind perceives polarities and relies on intuition. Meditation, a core component of Kundalini yoga, can help balance the neutral mind.

The Human Body

Your physical body serves as a temple. This is where the other nine bodies come together to coexist in peace. This body enables you to balance yourself and your life. You can also sacrifice your physical body for your ambitions, dreams, and community. The physical body contains the teacher's energy. It is kept in check by frequent exercise. The physical body likewise enjoys sharing what it has learned with others.

The Slope

Like a halo, your arcline body wraps around your head, earlobes, brow, and hairline. A second recline runs across your breast line if you are a woman. Your airline body permits you to sense the environment around you and project yourself onto it. This physique can assist you in focusing and meditating. Any practices related to the pituitary gland or the third eye (pineal gland) aid in waking the arcline body.

The Influence

Your aura body is the electromagnetic energy field that surrounds your physical body. It is in charge of storing your life force energy, shielding and protecting you. You can raise your vibration energetically and consciously by using your aura. Natural fibers used on the body, as well as meditation, help to awaken and balance your aura. You can also include white in your life and practice because it is thought to intensify and enlarge your aura.

The Pranic Self

Your breath, which carries life-force energy into your physical body, supports your pranic body. This gives you a sense of accomplishment and vigor in your life. Every time you breathe in and out, you engage with this body. Pranayama practices awaken and support the pranic body.

The Inconspicuous Body

Your subtle body is your ninth body, and it assists you in seeing beyond physical stuff and into what else exists. This body is inextricably linked to your soul body because it transports your soul body once your physical body dies. Despite no longer being in physical realization, many outstanding teachers and gurus continue to teach us through their subtle bodies. This body contains your potential to master anything. Do a Kundalini practice for 1,000 days if you wish to experience mastery. Your subtle body will then be balanced.

The Luminous Body

Your radiant body is your tenth and final body. This body is in charge of your luminosity, courage, and dignity. When you encounter someone who is inherently captivating and magnetic, you will notice that they have a well-balanced, glowing body. Commitment is required to balance and awaken your beautiful body. Balance and awaken your radiant body by being committed to your practice, truth, kindness, and perfection.

Embodiment

Though not strictly a body, embodiment is critical to awakening the ten bodies. Embodiment implies that all ten bodies have been awakened and are in equilibrium. This is Kundalini's ultimate goal. You awaken, balance, and strengthen your ten body when practicing Kundalini yoga.

Your Solar Plexus and Personal Pursuits

The energy provided by our Solar Plexus is the energy that assists us in finding and achieving success. It provides us with the fortitude we need to face challenges head-on. It inspires us to tackle circumstances with confidence and audacity, resulting in our success. However, sometimes, we struggle to channel the energy of the Solar Plexus, resulting in low self-esteem or lack of confidence. When we lack these critical components of success, the obstacles we face become larger, and our capacity to succeed appears impossible. Fortunately, our capacity to channel the

Solar Plexus' energy enhances our confidence and self-esteem, giving us the tools to succeed in our undertakings. So, if you notice your self-esteem, confidence, or self-worth disappearing or dissolving at a moment when you need it the most, do the following exercise:

Breathing with Authority

1. Make a mental note of the sensations you experience in your stomach and/or chest when you inhale and exhale right before or during a hard or nerve-racking circumstance. Is your breathing strong and confident? Or is there a tiny tremor?

2. Observe the shaking of your hands, the unsteady rise and fall of your chest as you breathe, or the uneasy sensations

that seem to dominate your stomach, if appropriate.

3. After you've done the above assessments, take charge of your breathing. On command, instruct your body to inhale and exhale slowly. Will your body's naturally automatic breathing action obey your command?

4. Consider: I have control over my body. My circumstances are under my control. I feel empowered. I am in command.

5. Maintain control of your breathing until all unsteadiness, shivering, and anxiousness have subsided. If you feel in control of your circumstances, you should be able to attack the problem with renewed or freshly discovered courage and confidence.

www.ingramcontent.com/pod-product-compliance
Lightning Source LLC
Chambersburg PA
CBHW052141110526
44591CB00012B/1815